UNVEILING
TOULOUSE

Your Travel Guide to The Pink City

ESSENTIALS EDITION

FRANCE UNVEILED SEARIES

Presented by

Discover Your Journey

a WEST AGORA INT S.R.L. Brand
www.tailoredtravelguides.com
Edited by WEST AGORA INT S.R.L.
WEST AGORA INT S.R.L. All Rights Reserved
Copyright © WEST AGORA INT S.R.L., 2023

West Agora Int

WIKI

Toulouse: The Pink City's Blend of Heritage, Innovation, and Vibrant Culture

Toulouse, affectionately known as "La Ville Rose" (The Pink City) for its distinctive terracotta brick architecture, is a city that harmoniously blends a rich historical heritage with modern innovation and a vibrant cultural scene. Located in the heart of southwestern France, Toulouse stands as a testament to the region's historical significance and its role as a hub of aerospace and technology.

Founded in the Roman era, Toulouse's strategic location along the Garonne River facilitated its growth as a major trading and cultural center. The city's history is deeply intertwined with the Occitan culture, and it played a pivotal role during the Albigensian Crusade in the early 13th century. This rich medieval past is evident in its historic architecture, including the Basilica of Saint-Sernin, one of Europe's largest Romanesque churches, and the stunning Capitole de Toulouse, the city's town hall and opera house, showcasing the grandeur of its civic architecture.

Toulouse is not just a city steeped in history; it is also a center of technological and scientific advancement, notably in the aerospace industry. Home to Airbus and the Cité de l'Espace (City of Space), Toulouse is at the forefront of space and aeronautical exploration, reflecting the city's innovative spirit.

The city's culinary scene mirrors its cultural richness, offering a blend of traditional Occitan and Southern French cuisine, with local specialties like cassoulet and Toulouse sausage. The vibrant markets, such as the Marché Victor Hugo, provide a taste of the region's gastronomic diversity.

Toulouse's commitment to arts and culture is evident in its numerous museums, galleries, and theaters. The Musée des Augustins, housing a fine collection of Romanesque and Gothic sculptures, and the contemporary Les Abattoirs museum, reflect the city's artistic diversity.

The city's urban landscape is a blend of historic charm and modern dynamism. The Garonne River and the Canal du Midi, a UNESCO World Heritage site, add to the city's picturesque setting, while modern infrastructure and public transport systems reflect its status as a growing metropolitan area.

Toulouse has been home to several notable figures, including the poet Pierre de Ronsard and the scientist Pierre-Paul Riquet, the engineer behind the Canal du Midi. The city's intellectual and cultural influence extends far beyond its borders, contributing significantly to the fields of literature, science, and the arts.

The city also boasts a vibrant student population, thanks to its prestigious universities and educational institutions. This youthful energy infuses the city with a dynamic and forward-looking spirit, evident in its lively nightlife, music scene, and numerous cultural festivals.

Toulouse's commitment to sustainability and green living is reflected in its well-maintained parks and gardens, such as the Jardin des Plantes and the Jardin Japonais, offering serene escapes within the urban landscape. The city's focus on eco-friendly initiatives and quality of life for its residents underscores its vision for a sustainable future.

Today, Toulouse stands as a city where tradition and modernity coexist in harmony. It offers a journey through time, where the echoes of the past blend with the innovations of the present. For those seeking to explore a city where history, technology, and vibrant culture converge, Toulouse presents a captivating and multifaceted experience.

CONTENTS

1 — GREETINGS AND RECOMMENDATIONS FROM LOCALS

PRACTICAL INFORMATION — 3

10 — TOP ATTRACTIONS IN TOULOUSE

HIDDEN GEMS AND LESSER-KNOWN SIGHTS IN TOULOUSE — 22

31 — PARKS AND GARDENS IN TOULOUSE

TOULOUSE'S CULINARY SCENE — 35

40 — SHOPPING IN TOULOUSE

FAMILY-FRIENDLY ACTIVITIES IN TOULOUSE — 43

46 — TOULOUSE BY NIGHT

ART AND CULTURE IN TOULOUSE — 58

62 — HISTORICAL AND ARCHITECTURAL LANDMARKS IN TOULOUSE

DAY TRIPS FROM TOULOUSE — 66

71 — END NOTE

TOULOUSE

THE PINK CITY

Toulouse, fondly known as 'La Ville Rose' (The Pink City) for its distinctive terracotta brick architecture, stands as a testament to both historic grandeur and contemporary dynamism. Nestled in the heart of the Occitanie region in southern France, this city is a harmonious blend of medieval charm and space-age technology. As you wander through its bustling streets, you will be captivated by the warmth of its pink buildings bathed in the golden southern French sun, and the vibrancy of its markets and cafes.

This guide invites you to explore Toulouse's enchanting streets, where history whispers from the walls of ancient churches and future dreams are shaped at the forefront of aerospace innovation. We will journey through its historic sites, savor its culinary delights, and uncover hidden gems. Toulouse, with its rich history, thriving cultural scene, and picturesque setting along the Garonne River, offers a unique experience for every traveler. Whether you are an art lover, a history enthusiast, or simply in search of a leisurely stroll along tree-lined canals, Toulouse will capture your heart.

Our guide is designed to provide a comprehensive and in-depth look at Toulouse, combining practical tips with cultural insights. We aim to make your visit to Toulouse not just a trip, but an experience filled with discovery and delight - where available, entries include fast access to official websites for easy booking and extra up-to-date information like prices, opening hours, availability, etc. Let's embark on this journey through Toulouse, a city where every corner holds a story waiting to be told.

GREETINGS AND INSIGHTS FROM LOCALS

Bienvenue, dear traveler! Welcome to Toulouse, the Pink City, where the bricks blush under the southern sun, and the spirit of innovation pulses through the winding streets. As a Toulousain, I've basked in the warmth of our city's vibrant culture and rich history, and I'm eager to share with you the charming nooks and exhilarating experiences that only a local would know.

Begin your Toulousain journey by embracing our convivial ambiance. A friendly "bonjour" and a warm smile will open up a world of discovery in this city of aerospace pioneers and medieval splendor, as you meander from the grand Place du Capitole to the enchanting banks of the Garonne.

You might find yourself enchanted by the Basilique Saint-Sernin, a marvel of Romanesque architecture. Here, amidst ancient relics and soaring arches, the basilica tells a story of Toulouse's devout heritage and architectural prowess, offering a peaceful retreat from the urban bustle.

For an immersion in our city's innovative spirit, head to the Cité de l'Espace. This space-themed park ignites the imagination with its planetarium, life-size rocket models, and interactive exhibits, celebrating Toulouse's pivotal role in the aerospace industry.

When the allure of local flavors calls, explore the Marché Victor Hugo. In this lively marketplace, indulge in the gastronomic delights of the Southwest – from succulent cassoulet to the rich foie gras. Here, each dish is a tribute to our region's gourmet heritage.

As dusk unfurls its rosy hues, the charm of the Quartier Saint-Cyprien beckons. This dynamic district, with its eclectic mix of galleries and cafes, pulses with the city's artistic heart, offering a perfect setting for an evening of cultural exploration and relaxation.

Along the river, the Pont Neuf, despite its name, stands as an age-old guardian of the city. Its majestic arches and enduring presence offer a moment of reflection on Toulouse's journey through time, from its Roman roots to its modern-day vibrancy.

Toulouse's essence lies in its harmonious blend of historical grandeur and contemporary innovation. We, the Toulousains, are here with open hearts, ready to share the allure and secrets of our beloved Ville Rose with you. À bientôt, dear traveler, and may your visit to Toulouse be as captivating and colorful as the city itself!

PRACTICAL INFORMATION

Currency Toulouse operates with the Euro (€). While credit and debit cards are widely accepted, carrying cash is recommended for small purchases, particularly in local markets. ATMs are readily available throughout the city for convenience.

Transportation Toulouse boasts a comprehensive and user-friendly public transportation system operated by Tisséo, encompassing buses, trams, and a metro service. This network provides seamless connectivity to all major attractions and neighborhoods. For those who prefer exploring at a slower pace, Toulouse is a pedestrian-friendly city with numerous walking routes and a robust bike-sharing program - VélôToulouse, offering a scenic and eco-friendly way to see the city. Additionally, visitors can enjoy boat tours along the Canal du Midi and Garonne River, providing unique perspectives of the city's picturesque landscapes and historic architecture.

Driving Driving in Toulouse can be a convenient option for visiting nearby attractions outside the city. However, within the city center, it's advisable to use public transportation or walk, as many areas are pedestrianized and parking can be scarce and expensive. Traffic can be heavy during peak hours, and some of the historic areas have narrow, one-way streets that require careful navigation. Car rental services are available at the airport and throughout the city for those wishing to explore the broader Occitanie region.

PRACTICAL INFORMATION

Climate Toulouse enjoys a temperate climate. Summers are typically warm and sunny, perfect for outdoor activities, while winters are mild with occasional rain. Spring and autumn offer moderate temperatures and fewer tourists, making them ideal times to explore the city's outdoor attractions and beautiful parks.

Language French is the primary language spoken in Toulouse. Basic knowledge of French is useful, although English is commonly spoken in tourist areas.

Power sockets and adapters France uses Type E power sockets, with a standard voltage of 230V and a frequency of 50Hz. Travelers should bring a suitable adapter for their devices.

Shopping Toulouse's shopping scene ranges from trendy boutiques in Quartier Saint-Georges to unique finds along Rue Saint-Rome. The bustling Marché Victor Hugo offers local specialties. Shops generally open from 10 AM to 7 PM, with a pause in the afternoon. Sunday shopping is limited.

Tipping Tipping in Toulouse is customary but not mandatory. Service charges are often included in restaurant bills, but an additional tip of 5-10% is appreciated for excellent service. For taxi services, rounding up the fare or adding a small tip is a common practice among locals and tourists.

PRACTICAL INFORMATION

USEFUL LINKS AND PHONE NUMBERS

Emergency Services
All Emergencies: 112
Police: 17
Fire Brigade: 18
Medical Emergencies (SAMU): 15

Transportation
Toulouse-Blagnac Airport: +33 825 380 000, www.toulouse.aeroport.fr/en
SNCF (French National Railway Company): +33 9 70 60 99 70, www.sncf.com/en
Tisséo (Public Transport in Toulouse): +33 5 61 41 70 70, www.tisseo.fr/en
Bike-sharing program, VélôToulouse https://abo-toulouse.cyclocity.fr/

Tourist Information
Toulouse Tourism Office: +33 892 180 180, www.toulouse-visit.com
Toulouse City Pass www.toulouse-visit.com/pass-tourisme

Hospitals
Toulouse University Hospital: +33 5 61 77 22 33, www.chu-toulouse.fr

Local Government
City of Toulouse: +33 5 61 22 29 22, https://metropole.toulouse.fr/

Maps

For print versions - quick acces through QR codes after the End Note

Toulouse maps: www.ontheworldmap.com/france/city/toulouse/
Toulouse Detailed Street Map:
www.ontheworldmap.com/france/city/toulouse/large-detailed-map-of-toulouse.jpg
Toulouse Tourist Map:
www.ontheworldmap.com/france/city/toulouse/toulouse-tourist-attractions-map.jpg
Toulouse Sightseeing Map:
www.ontheworldmap.com/france/city/toulouse/toulouse-sightseeing-map.jpg
Toulouse 10 must-see-sites Map:
www.ontheworldmap.com/france/city/toulouse/toulouse-10-must-see-sites-map.jpg
Toulouse Bike Lanes Map
https://metropole.toulouse.fr/sites/toulouse-fr/files/2022-08/gdtlsevelodpltverso2020web.pdf
Toulouse City Center Map:
www.ontheworldmap.com/france/city/toulouse/toulouse-city-center-map.jpg
Toulouse Transport Map:
www.ontheworldmap.com/france/city/toulouse/toulouse-transport-map.jpg
Toulouse Metro and Tam Map:
www.ontheworldmap.com/france/city/toulouse/toulouse-metro-and-tram-map.jp

PRACTICAL INFORMATION
TOULOUSE AND SURROUNDINGS

Free high resolution & download at: www.openstreetmap.org/#map=13/43.6025/1.4134 Copyright @ OpenStreetMaps

PRACTICAL INFORMATION
TOULOUSE AND SURROUNDINGS

Free high resolution & download at: www.openstreetmap.org/#map=13/43.6025/1.4134 Copyright @ OpenStreetMaps

TOULOUSE CITY MAP

Free high resolution & download at: https://www.openstreetmap.org/#map=15/43.6018/1.4279 Copyright @ OpenStreetMaps

TOULOUSE CITY MAP

Free high resolution & download at: https://www.openstreetmap.org/#map=15/43.6018/1.4279 Copyright @ OpenStreetMaps

TOP ATTRACTIONS IN TOULOUSE

BASILIQUE SAINT-SERNIN

The Basilique Saint-Sernin stands as a majestic beacon of Romanesque architecture in the heart of Toulouse. Esteemed as one of the largest Romanesque churches in Europe, it boasts a history that dates back to the 11th century. The basilica, a designated UNESCO World Heritage Site, is an integral part of the Santiago de Compostela pilgrimage route. Its captivating structure is adorned with intricately detailed sculptures and a striking octagonal bell tower that dominates the Toulouse skyline.

Visitors are often mesmerized by the basilica's serene ambience and the exquisite artistry of its chapels and cloisters. Inside, the crypt houses a rich collection of relics, while the ambulatory and radiating chapels exemplify Romanesque grandeur. The basilica also features an impressive organ, which often fills the space with enchanting music, enhancing the spiritual and historical atmosphere.

Tip: To fully appreciate the basilica's architectural splendor, consider joining a guided tour. These tours often reveal hidden details and stories about the basilica's past, providing a deeper understanding of its significance and history. Additionally, try to visit during an organ concert for an unforgettable auditory experience.

Address: 7 Pl. Saint-Sernin, 31000 Toulouse, France
Website: https://basilique-saint-sernin.fr/

PLACE DU CAPITOLE

Place du Capitole, the vibrant heart of Toulouse, is more than just a public square; it's a symbol of the city's rich history and bustling present. Dominated by the grandiose Capitole building, which houses the city hall and the esteemed Théâtre du Capitole opera company, this expansive square is a hub of activity and culture. The façade of the Capitole, stretching 135 meters, is a magnificent example of neoclassical architecture, adorned with eight pink marble columns that epitomize Toulouse's nickname, "La Ville Rose." The square is a lively gathering place for both locals and tourists, offering a variety of cafes, restaurants, and shops in its vicinity. It's also the site of frequent markets and public events, including open-air concerts and seasonal festivals. The ground of the square, beautifully paved in Occitan cross design, invites visitors to stroll and soak in the vibrant atmosphere.

Tip: Be sure to visit the Salle des Illustres inside the Capitole building, known for its splendid frescoes and paintings depicting moments in Toulouse's history. Access is free, but the hall is occasionally closed for official events, so it's best to check the schedule in advance. Also, visiting the square early in the morning or late in the evening provides a more peaceful experience, allowing a better appreciation of its architectural beauty.

Address: Place du Capitole, 31000 Toulouse, France
Website: www.toulouse-visit.com/le-capitole

CITÉ DE L'ESPACE

Cité de l'Espace, located on the eastern outskirts of Toulouse, is a must-visit for space enthusiasts and curious minds. This unique space-themed park offers an immersive journey into the cosmos, blending education and entertainment. The park is renowned for its interactive exhibits, life-size spacecraft replicas, and engaging activities that bring the wonders of space exploration to life.

Visitors can marvel at a life-size model of the Ariane 5 rocket, walk through a replica of the Mir space station, and experience the thrill of a simulated space mission. The park also boasts a state-of-the-art planetarium, where you can journey through the stars and learn about the universe in stunning detail. The IMAX cinema adds another dimension to the experience, with breathtaking space documentaries that captivate audiences of all ages.

Tip: Allocate a full day to truly enjoy all that Cité de l'Espace has to offer. The park is vast, and its exhibits are both indoors and outdoors, so dress appropriately for the weather. Don't miss the observatory, which offers a chance to view celestial objects through a powerful telescope, especially during evening openings. Buying tickets online in advance can save time and sometimes offers a discount.

Address: Av. Jean Gonord, 31500 Toulouse, France
Website: https://en.cite-espace.com/

MUSÉE DES AUGUSTINS

The Musée des Augustins, nestled in the heart of Toulouse, is a treasure trove of art and history. Housed in a stunning 14th-century Gothic convent, this museum boasts an impressive collection of sculptures and paintings, spanning from the Middle Ages to the early 20th century. The serene cloisters and the majestic church of the former Augustinian monastery provide a fitting backdrop for the artworks displayed.

Visitors can explore rooms filled with Romanesque sculptures, a vast array of paintings from the Renaissance to the French Revolution, and more recent works by artists of the 19th and early 20th centuries. Notable highlights include masterpieces by Toulouse-Lautrec and Delacroix. The museum's sculpture garden, with its tranquil setting and remarkable stone carvings, offers a peaceful retreat within the bustling city.

Tip: The museum regularly hosts temporary exhibitions and cultural events, so check their schedule before your visit to catch special displays or guided tours. On the first Sunday of each month, entry to the museum is free, making it an excellent opportunity for art lovers on a budget. Additionally, don't miss the opportunity to experience one of their unique nighttime openings, where the museum's atmosphere is transformed by special lighting, adding a magical dimension to the artworks.

Address: 21 Rue de Metz, 31000 Toulouse, France
Website: www.augustins.org

CANAL DU MIDI

The Canal du Midi, a UNESCO World Heritage Site, is an engineering marvel and a picturesque waterway that flows through Toulouse. This 17th-century canal, stretching over 240 kilometers, was originally constructed to connect the Atlantic Ocean with the Mediterranean Sea. Today, it offers a serene escape in the heart of the city, lined with plane trees and traversed by charming old bridges and lock houses.

A stroll or bike ride along the canal's towpaths is a delightful way to experience Toulouse's natural beauty and tranquility. The path runs through the city and into the lush countryside, offering both leisurely walks and opportunities for more extensive cycling trips. Visitors can also enjoy boat tours, which provide a unique perspective of the city and the surrounding landscapes from the water.

Tip: For a truly memorable experience, consider renting a self-operated boat for a day or even a few days to explore the canal at your own pace. No boating license is required for these vessels. Alternatively, join a guided boat tour to learn more about the canal's fascinating history and significance. Pack a picnic to enjoy on the banks or stop at one of the canal-side restaurants for a leisurely meal with scenic views.

Address: Canal du Midi passes through multiple locations in Toulouse. One popular starting point is Port Saint-Sauveur, 31000 Toulouse, France.
Website: www.canal-du-midi.com/en

PONT NEUF

Pont Neuf, despite its name meaning "New Bridge" in French, is actually the oldest bridge in Toulouse, dating back to the 16th century. Spanning the Garonne River, this historic bridge is an architectural gem and a symbol of the city's rich past. With its unique oval-shaped arches designed to withstand the river's strong currents and floods, Pont Neuf is not only a feat of engineering but also a testament to the resilience and ingenuity of the era.

At night, the bridge is beautifully illuminated, creating a mesmerizing reflection on the water and offering a romantic backdrop for evening strolls. It connects the heart of Toulouse to the left bank, offering spectacular views of the river, the city's historic buildings, and the distant Pyrenees on clear days. The bridge itself is a popular spot for both locals and tourists to gather, relax, and enjoy the scenic surroundings.

Tip: For a stunning panoramic view, visit the bridge at sunset or during the early evening. This is when the lighting is ideal for photography, capturing the golden hues of the sunset or the city lights reflecting on the river. Also, consider taking a boat tour that passes under the bridge for a different perspective of this iconic structure.

Address: Pont Neuf, 31000 Toulouse, France
Website:
https://en.wikipedia.org/wiki/Pont_Neuf,_Toulouse

FONDATION BEMBERG

Fondation Bemberg is an exquisite art museum located in the heart of Toulouse, within the splendid Hôtel d'Assézat, a Renaissance mansion that is a work of art in itself. This museum is the legacy of art collector Georges Bemberg, who transformed his personal collection into a public treasure. The collection primarily focuses on art from the Renaissance to the 20th century, including paintings, sculptures, and decorative arts.

The exhibits showcase an impressive array of works by renowned artists such as Picasso, Matisse, and Toulouse-Lautrec, alongside masterpieces from the Renaissance period. Each room is thoughtfully curated, creating an intimate and immersive experience. The Fondation also frequently hosts temporary exhibitions, lectures, and concerts, adding to its cultural richness.

Tip: Take advantage of the audio guides available at the museum; they offer insightful commentary on the artworks and the history of the collection, enhancing your visit. The Fondation Bemberg is less crowded during weekdays, making it an ideal time for a more relaxed exploration of the galleries. After your museum visit, take a moment to enjoy the courtyard of the Hôtel d'Assézat, a peaceful spot that reflects the elegance of Toulouse's Renaissance architecture.

Address: Place d'Assézat, 31000 Toulouse, France
Website: www.fondation-bemberg.fr

HÔTEL D'ASSÉZAT

Hôtel d'Assézat in Toulouse is a stunning example of Renaissance architecture and a testament to the city's affluent past. Constructed in the 16th century for the wealthy merchant Pierre d'Assézat, this grand mansion now houses the Fondation Bemberg and is a cornerstone of cultural life in Toulouse. Its elegant façade, adorned with intricate carvings and sculptures, is a remarkable sight that captures the artistic spirit of the Renaissance.

The building's interior is equally impressive, featuring a spacious courtyard surrounded by ornate arches and columns. The Hôtel d'Assézat is not only admired for its architectural beauty but also for the rich art collection of the Fondation Bemberg, which it has been home to since 1994. This collection includes works from the Renaissance to the 20th century, offering a glimpse into various artistic movements and styles.

Tip: While visiting the Hôtel d'Assézat, take time to explore the courtyard and the building's architecture. It's a perfect spot for photography enthusiasts. Additionally, check the Fondation Bemberg's schedule for temporary exhibitions and cultural events held within the Hôtel, which often enhance the visitor experience with unique artistic displays and insights.

Address: Place d'Assézat, 31000 Toulouse, France
Website: www.fondation-bemberg.fr

LES ABATTOIRS

Les Abattoirs, located on the banks of the Garonne River in Toulouse, is a dynamic hub of contemporary art and culture. This modern art museum, set in a converted 19th-century slaughterhouse, represents a striking example of urban regeneration and cultural innovation. The space itself, with its industrial architecture, provides a unique backdrop for the exhibitions and artworks displayed.

The museum's collection focuses on modern and contemporary art from the 20th and 21st centuries, showcasing a wide range of mediums and styles. It features works by renowned international artists as well as emerging talents, offering a diverse and ever-changing artistic experience. Les Abattoirs is also known for its large-scale murals and installations, including a remarkable tapestry by Picasso.

Beyond the permanent collection, the museum hosts temporary exhibitions, live performances, and educational workshops, making it a lively center for artistic exploration and discourse.

Tip: Make sure to visit the museum's rooftop terrace, which offers a panoramic view of the Garonne River and Toulouse's cityscape. It's a perfect spot to relax and reflect after exploring the exhibits. Also, check the museum's calendar for special events and temporary exhibitions, which often feature cutting-edge contemporary artists and offer fresh perspectives on current artistic trends.

Address: 76 All. Charles de Fitte, 31300 Toulouse, France

Website: www.lesabattoirs.org/en

JARDIN JAPONAIS

Jardin Japonais, or the Japanese Garden, is a serene oasis nestled in the bustling Compans Caffarelli district of Toulouse. Designed in the style of a traditional Japanese garden, this tranquil space is a delightful escape from the city's hustle and bustle. Covering an area of approximately 7,000 square meters, it was created to symbolize the strong cultural ties between Toulouse and Japan.

The garden features all the classic elements of Japanese landscape design, including a picturesque pond with koi fish, a red bridge, a tea pavilion, and meticulously pruned plants and trees. The carefully arranged stones, water features, and lanterns all contribute to the peaceful atmosphere. It's a place for contemplation, relaxation, and connecting with nature.

Visitors can stroll along the winding paths, enjoy the changing seasons reflected in the flora, or simply sit and appreciate the calm environment. The garden is particularly beautiful during the cherry blossom season when the trees are in full bloom.

Tip: The garden is a perfect spot for photographers and nature lovers. Visit early in the morning or late in the afternoon for fewer crowds and softer light, ideal for photography. The garden also hosts occasional cultural events related to Japanese traditions, which are a great opportunity to deepen your understanding of Japanese culture.

Address: Jardin Compans Caffarelli, Bd Lascrosses, 31000 Toulouse,
Website: www.toulouse-visit.com/jardin-japonais/toulouse/pcumid031fs0007f

MUSÉE SAINT-RAYMOND

Musée Saint-Raymond, set in the vibrant heart of Toulouse, is a museum dedicated to archaeology and antiquities, particularly from the Roman period. Located adjacent to the Basilique Saint-Sernin, this museum is housed in a former university college dating back to the 16th century, offering a perfect blend of historical architecture and intriguing exhibits.

The museum's collection is primarily focused on the classical antiquities from the Toulouse region, including a remarkable array of Roman sculptures, ceramics, and other artifacts. One of the highlights is the extensive collection of Roman busts and statues, some of which were discovered in nearby ancient villas and public buildings. The museum also offers insights into the lives of the Gallo-Roman citizens of ancient Tolosa (now Toulouse), showcasing everyday objects, jewelry, and tools.

The lower level of the museum reveals the foundations of a Roman necropolis, providing a unique glimpse into ancient burial practices and beliefs. Interactive displays and multimedia installations make the ancient world come alive for visitors of all ages.

Tip: Don't miss the museum's temporary exhibitions, which often explore various aspects of ancient history and archaeology in more depth. The museum is particularly engaging for families, offering educational workshops and activities for children. Additionally, the museum's terrace offers a beautiful view of the Basilique Saint-Sernin, perfect for a scenic break.

Address: 1 ter Pl. Saint-Sernin, 31000 Toulouse, France
Website: https://saintraymond.toulouse.fr/

COUVENT DES JACOBINS

The Couvent des Jacobins, a jewel of Gothic architecture in Toulouse, is renowned for its remarkable history and architectural beauty. Originally built in the 13th century as a Dominican convent, this historic monument now serves as a museum and cultural venue. Its serene cloisters, majestic church, and peaceful garden offer a glimpse into the medieval ecclesiastical life.

Visitors are often captivated by the church's stunning vaulted ceilings, particularly the "Palm Tree" column, a unique architectural feature resembling a palm tree, from which ribbed vaults spread outwards. The convent's halls and chapels are adorned with medieval frescoes and religious art, creating an atmosphere of contemplative tranquility.

The convent is also the final resting place of Saint Thomas Aquinas, making it an important pilgrimage site. The Jacobins' refectory and chapter house, now used for exhibitions and events, add to the site's historical richness.

Tip: Take the time to visit during one of the classical music concerts frequently held in the church. The acoustics in the Gothic structure are exceptional, providing an unforgettable auditory experience. Additionally, the convent offers guided tours, which can greatly enhance your understanding of the site's history and architectural significance. The peaceful cloister garden is a perfect spot to relax and reflect after exploring the convent.

Address: Pl. des Jacobins, 31000 Toulouse, France
Website: https://jacobins.toulouse.fr/

HIDDEN GEMS AND LESSER-KNOWN SIGHTS IN TOULOUSE

CHAPELLE DES CARMÉLITES

The Chapelle des Carmélites, tucked away in the heart of Toulouse, is a hidden gem that boasts an extraordinary interior, often surprising visitors with its artistic richness. Originally part of a Carmelite convent, this small chapel, dating back to the 17th century, is a masterpiece of Baroque art.

The chapel's walls and ceiling are adorned with magnificent frescoes, depicting scenes from the Old and New Testaments, along with various saints and biblical figures. These vibrant paintings, created by Jean-Pierre Rivalz and Antoine Durand, envelop the entire interior, offering an immersive and awe-inspiring visual experience. The contrast between the chapel's unassuming exterior and its opulent interior is striking.

Tip: Due to its relatively hidden location and modest exterior, the Chapelle des Carmélites is easy to miss. Look for the discreet entrance on Rue du Périgord. Visiting this chapel is best combined with a leisurely walk around the neighborhood, allowing you to discover more of Toulouse's historical and architectural treasures. The chapel is often quiet, making it an ideal spot for contemplation and admiration of the Baroque artistry.

Address: 1 Rue de Périgord, 31000 Toulouse, France
Website: www.toulouse-visit.com/chapelle-des-carmelites/toulouse/pcumid031fs00094

MUSÉE GEORGES LABIT

The Musée Georges Labit is a unique museum in Toulouse, dedicated to Asian and Egyptian art and artifacts. Situated in a Moorish villa surrounded by a lush Mediterranean and exotic garden, this museum offers a fascinating journey through ancient civilizations. Founded in 1893, it was one of the first museums in France to present art from these distant cultures.

The collection includes a wide array of Asian art, encompassing pieces from India, China, Japan, and other Asian countries. The Egyptian section houses an impressive collection of artifacts, including mummies, sarcophagi, and everyday objects, offering insights into the life and beliefs of ancient Egyptians. The museum's setting in a charming villa adds to the allure, creating a sense of being transported to another time and place.

Tip: Be sure to explore the museum's garden, which is as much a part of the experience as the exhibits themselves. The garden features a variety of plants and trees from the regions represented in the museum, along with a peaceful pond. It's a perfect place to relax and reflect after your visit. The museum also hosts temporary exhibitions and cultural events, so check their schedule to see what special events might coincide with your visit.

Address: 17 Rue du Japon, 31400 Toulouse, France
Website: www.museegeorgeslabit.fr

RUE SAINT-ROME

Rue Saint-Rome, a vibrant and historic street in the heart of Toulouse, offers a delightful exploration experience away from the typical tourist paths. Stretching through the city's center, this pedestrianized street is a lively blend of history, culture, and commerce. With buildings dating back to the Middle Ages, it encapsulates the city's rich architectural heritage.

As you stroll down Rue Saint-Rome, you'll find an array of boutique shops, local artisan stores, and charming cafes. The street is known for its unique and eclectic shopping experience, ranging from vintage clothing and jewelry to traditional French products and contemporary fashion. The bustling atmosphere is accentuated by street musicians and artists, adding a lively and authentic touch to your walk.

Rue Saint-Rome is not only a shopping destination but also a window into the daily life of Toulouse. The street's narrowness and old buildings give it a distinctly medieval feel, inviting visitors to imagine the city's past.

Tip: Plan to visit Rue Saint-Rome on a weekday morning or early afternoon when the street is less crowded, allowing for a more relaxed shopping and exploration experience. Don't hesitate to venture into the smaller side streets branching off from Rue Saint-Rome, where you can discover hidden cafes and quaint boutiques.

Address: Rue Saint-Rome, 31000 Toulouse, France
Website: www.toulouse-tournages.fr/rue-saint-rome

HÔTEL DE BERNUY

Hôtel de Bernuy, a hidden architectural gem in Toulouse, stands as a magnificent example of the city's Renaissance heritage. Built in the early 16th century for Jean de Bernuy, a wealthy merchant of pastel, a plant dye that brought prosperity to the region, this grand mansion is a testament to the affluence of its time.

The building is renowned for its striking Gothic façade and its remarkable spiral staircase housed in an octagonal tower, a feature that showcases the transition from Gothic to Renaissance styles. The staircase, visible from the courtyard, is a masterpiece of stone craftsmanship. The Hôtel de Bernuy also boasts intricate sculptures and detailed Renaissance decorations that adorn its exterior.

Today, this historical building houses the prestigious Lycée Pierre de Fermat, making its interior less accessible to the public. However, its exterior alone makes it worth a visit.

Tip: Although the interior of Hôtel de Bernuy is not generally open to the public, the building's exterior is best appreciated in the soft light of the early morning or late afternoon. These times offer the perfect lighting for photography enthusiasts looking to capture the intricate details of the façade and the towering beauty of its spiral staircase. Additionally, the surrounding area is rich in historical sites, making it ideal for a walking tour of Toulouse's Renaissance architecture.

Address: 1 Rue Léon Gambetta, 31000 Toulouse, France
Website: www.toulouse-visit.com/hotel-de-bernuy/toulouse/pcumid031fs0098w

CHÂTEAU D'EAU

Château d'Eau, originally an 18th-century water tower, stands today as one of Toulouse's most distinctive landmarks and a premier venue for photography exhibitions. This unique circular building, located near the banks of the Garonne River, was ingeniously repurposed in the 1970s to become one of the first public galleries dedicated exclusively to photography in France.

The structure itself is architecturally fascinating, with its robust brick construction and distinctive cylindrical shape. Inside, the gallery spans several levels, offering a spiraling journey through contemporary and historical photographic works. Exhibitions here are thoughtfully curated, featuring a mix of renowned international photographers and emerging talents, making it a must-visit for art and photography enthusiasts.

Beyond its exhibitions, Château d'Eau is celebrated for its contribution to the photographic arts, hosting workshops, lectures, and events that engage the community and foster a deeper appreciation for the medium.

Tip: After your visit, take a leisurely walk along the nearby Garonne River for picturesque views of Toulouse. The area around Château d'Eau, especially at sunset, offers some of the most photogenic scenes in the city. Check the gallery's schedule in advance, as they frequently host special events and new exhibition openings, which are often accompanied by talks or guided tours, providing richer insights into the showcased works.

Address: 1 Pl. Laganne, 31300 Toulouse, France
Website: https://chateaudeau.toulouse.fr/en/

LE BAZACLE

Le Bazacle, positioned on the banks of the Garonne River in Toulouse, offers a unique blend of history, culture, and nature. This site, originally a ford crossing and later transformed into a series of water mills in the Middle Ages, has evolved into a multipurpose space that includes an exhibition center, a fish pass, and beautiful terraces overlooking the river.

Managed by EDF (Électricité de France), Le Bazacle provides an insightful look into the history of hydroelectric power in the region. The exhibition center features interactive displays and educational panels explaining the development and functioning of hydroelectricity. This fusion of industrial heritage with educational content makes it a fascinating visit for those interested in science and environmental studies.

One of the highlights of Le Bazacle is its outdoor terrace, offering stunning views of the river and the cityscape. It's a perfect spot for photography or simply relaxing by the water.

Tip: Plan your visit to coincide with one of the temporary art exhibitions often hosted at Le Bazacle, which add an artistic dimension to the experience. Also, the outdoor terrace is an ideal location for bird watching, particularly during the migration season. Check the EDF website for the schedule of events and exhibitions, which can enhance your visit with additional cultural and educational experiences.

Address: Quai de l'Exil Républicain Espagnol, 1, 31000 Toulouse, France

Website: www.toulouse-visit.com/espaces-edf-bazacle/toulouse/pcumid031fs0003b

QUARTIER SAINT-CYPRIEN

Quartier Saint-Cyprien, located on the left bank of the Garonne River in Toulouse, is a vibrant and eclectic neighborhood often overlooked by tourists. This district, with its mix of historic charm and modern energy, offers a more authentic slice of Toulouse life. The area is known for its diverse cultural scene, bustling markets, and a range of dining options, from traditional French bistros to international cuisine.

The heart of Saint-Cyprien is its market, Marché Saint-Cyprien, where locals shop for fresh produce, cheese, and other regional specialties. The streets around the market are lined with independent shops, art galleries, and cafes, making it a delightful area to explore on foot. The neighborhood also boasts significant cultural institutions like Les Abattoirs, a modern art museum, and La Grave hospital, known for its iconic dome.

The architecture in Saint-Cyprien ranges from medieval to contemporary, reflecting the area's long and varied history. The district's relaxed atmosphere is especially evident in its small parks and along the riverbank, where residents enjoy leisurely strolls and picnics.

Tip: Visit Quartier Saint-Cyprien on a Saturday morning to experience the lively atmosphere of the weekly market. It's a great opportunity to sample local foods and interact with residents. In the evening, explore the neighborhood's vibrant bar and restaurant scene, offering a more local and less touristy nightlife experience compared to the city center.

Address: Quartier Saint-Cyprien, 31300 Toulouse, France
Website: www.toulouse-visit.com/emblematic-quarters

TOULOUSE OBSERVATORY

The Toulouse Observatory, an astronomical observatory located in the heart of the city, is a hidden gem for space enthusiasts and curious minds alike. Established in the 18th century, it is one of the oldest observatories in France and has played a significant role in the development of astronomy and space science. The observatory is part of the Observatoire Midi-Pyrénées (OMP), which contributes to various fields of astrophysics and Earth sciences.

Visitors to the Toulouse Observatory can delve into the world of astronomy through guided tours and educational activities. The observatory houses historic telescopes and instruments, offering a glimpse into the evolution of astronomical research. The site also includes a beautifully maintained garden, adding to its charm and making it a peaceful retreat within the city.

The observatory actively participates in research and education, making it a valuable resource for both the scientific community and the public. Its outreach programs aim to make astronomy accessible to all, fostering a deeper appreciation for the wonders of the universe.

Tip: Check the observatory's schedule for public events, such as night sky observations, lectures, and special exhibitions. These events often provide unique opportunities to look through telescopes and learn from experts, making for an educational and memorable experience. Visiting during special astronomical events, like meteor showers or eclipses, can be particularly fascinating.

Address: Jardin de l'Observatoire, 1 Av. Camille Flammarion, 31500 Toulouse, France
Website: https://saptoulouse.net/

L'HÔTEL DAHUS

L'Hôtel Dahus, a lesser-known yet captivating historical site in Toulouse, is an exquisite example of Renaissance architecture. Located in the charming neighborhood of Dalbade, this 16th-century mansion is renowned for its unique and mysterious façade adorned with sculpted wooden heads, known as "dahus." These mythical creature figures lend an air of intrigue and whimsy to the building's exterior.

The mansion's architecture reflects the prosperity and artistic flourish of Toulouse during the Renaissance era. Its detailed stone work, ornate windows, and grand entrance all contribute to its historical significance. While the interior of L'Hôtel Dahus is not regularly open to the public, its exterior is a visual treat and a testament to the skill of Renaissance craftsmen.

L'Hôtel Dahus is nestled among narrow streets lined with other historical buildings, making it part of a picturesque and often overlooked area of Toulouse. A stroll around this neighborhood reveals a quiet, more authentic side of the city.

Tip: To fully appreciate the history and details of L'Hôtel Dahus, consider taking a guided walking tour of the Dalbade neighborhood. These tours often provide fascinating insights into the history and legends surrounding the building and its unique façade. The area is also perfect for photography enthusiasts looking to capture the essence of Toulouse's Renaissance period.

Address: 9 Rue Théodore Ozenne Toulouse, France
Website: www.pop.culture.gouv.fr/notice/merimee/PA00094539

PARKS AND GARDENS IN TOULOUSE

JARDIN DES PLANTES

Jardin des Plantes in Toulouse is not just a garden, but a lively park filled with a rich variety of flora, historical statues, and winding pathways. Spanning over seven hectares, this historic park, established in the 18th century, is a blend of botanical garden and urban park. It offers a peaceful retreat with its beautifully landscaped grounds, thematic gardens, and large trees providing ample shade.

The park is also a haven for families and children, featuring playgrounds, a carousel, and even a small zoo with domestic animals. The garden's duck pond and charming bridges add to its picturesque setting. Throughout the year, Jardin des Plantes hosts various events, including outdoor concerts and exhibitions, making it a cultural hotspot in the city.

Tip: Visit the Jardin des Plantes during spring when the flowerbeds and trees are in full bloom, offering a stunning display of colors and fragrances. It's also a perfect time for photography enthusiasts. For a complete experience, bring along a picnic and enjoy a leisurely afternoon amidst the natural beauty of the park.

Address: 31 All. Jules Guesde, 31400 Toulouse, France
Website: https://metropole.toulouse.fr/annuaire/jardin-des-plantes

JARDIN ROYAL

Jardin Royal in Toulouse, the city's oldest public garden established in 1754, is a splendid example of classic French garden design. Its historical significance and beautifully manicured landscapes make it a serene sanctuary in the urban setting. Spanning a considerable area, this elegant park is meticulously arranged with symmetrical trees, vibrant flower beds, and neatly trimmed hedges, embodying the charm and sophistication of traditional French gardens.

As you wander through its paths, you'll encounter charming features like a picturesque pond, home to ducks and swans, and several ornate statues enhancing the garden's aesthetic appeal. The central gazebo, often a venue for musicians, adds a romantic ambience, especially during impromptu performances. The park's layout encourages leisurely strolls, peaceful relaxation, and picnics under the shade of ancient trees.

Jardin Royal is not just a place of natural beauty but also a cultural retreat, where locals and tourists alike can immerse themselves in the tranquility of nature while being in the heart of the city. Its benches, strategically placed throughout the garden, offer spots to sit and admire the surrounding beauty or indulge in a good book.

Tip: The garden is particularly enchanting in the early morning when the light is soft, and the atmosphere is most tranquil. It's a perfect time for photographers or those seeking a quiet moment. Additionally, visiting in spring allows you to witness the splendid bloom of flowers, adding a burst of color to the already picturesque setting.

Address: Angle Rue Ozenne et Allées Jules Guesde, 31000 Toulouse, France

Website: https://metropole.toulouse.fr/annuaire/jardin-royal

GRAND ROND PARK

Grand Rond Park, also known as Jardin du Grand Rond, is a circular park in Toulouse characterized by its unique layout and variety of plants. This historic park, dating back to the 18th century, features beautifully landscaped gardens, statues, and a central fountain. It's a peaceful haven for nature lovers and those seeking a quiet escape.

Tip: Enjoy a leisurely walk through the interconnected gardens of Grand Rond, Jardin Royal, and Jardin des Plantes, all part of a larger green corridor. The park is especially beautiful in spring with blooming flowers.

Address: Rond-point Boulingrin, 31000 Toulouse, France
Website: www.toulouse-visit.com/jardin-du-grand-rond/toulouse/pcumid031fs0007b

PARC DE LA PRAIRIE DES FILTRES

Parc de la Prairie des Filtres, situated along the Garonne River, is a popular green space in Toulouse known for its scenic views and spacious lawns. This park, a favorite among locals, is perfect for picnics, sports, and leisurely strolls along the riverbank. It hosts various events and festivals, adding to its lively atmosphere. The park's name originates from its historical use for filtering drinking water.

Tip: Visit during sunset for spectacular views of the Garonne River against the backdrop of the Toulouse skyline. It's also an ideal spot for outdoor activities like jogging or playing frisbee.

Address: Cr Dillon, 31300 Toulouse, France
Website: www.toulouse-visit.com/prairie-des-filtres/toulouse/pcumid031v5014kz

PARC DU RAMIER

Parc du Ramier, located on an island in the Garonne River, offers a vast green space ideal for various outdoor activities. This park features walking paths, sports facilities, and ample open areas for picnics and relaxation. Its unique setting on the river provides a refreshing and natural environment within the city.

Tip: Take advantage of the park's sports fields for a game of soccer or rugby. The park's river setting also makes it a great spot for a scenic jog or walk.

Address: Île du Ramier, 31400 Toulouse, France
Website: https://metropole.toulouse.fr/actualites/amenagement-ile-du-ramier

PARC FONTAINE LESTANG - LA BISCOTTE

Parc Fontaine Lestang, affectionately known as "La Biscotte," is a quaint and charming park located in the Fontaine Lestang neighborhood of Toulouse. This small but delightful green space offers a peaceful retreat with its well-manicured gardens, shaded areas, and a lovely central fountain. It's an ideal spot for locals and visitors to relax, read, or enjoy a quiet stroll. The park also features a playground, making it a favorite among families with young children. **Tip**: Bring a book or a picnic to enjoy a leisurely afternoon in this serene setting. The park's intimate size and tranquil atmosphere make it a perfect place for unwinding away from the city's busier areas.

Address: Rue d'Auch, 31100 Toulouse, France
Website: www.pres-dici.com/sorties/parc-fontaine-lestang/

TOULOUSE CULINARY SCENE

MICHEL SARRAN

Michel Sarran is an esteemed Michelin-starred restaurant located in the heart of Toulouse. Led by the acclaimed chef Michel Sarran, the restaurant is celebrated for its creative and refined approach to French cuisine. The dishes are a blend of traditional flavors and modern techniques, presented with artistic flair. The interior exudes elegance and warmth, providing a perfect setting for a memorable gastronomic experience. **Tip**: Reserve in advance, as this popular spot fills up quickly. For a truly special experience, opt for the chef's tasting menu, which showcases the best of his culinary artistry.

Address: 21 Bd Armand Duportal, 31000 Toulouse, France
Website: www.michel-sarran.com/en/

LA GOURMANDINE

La Gourmandine, situated in Toulouse's bustling city center, is a charming bistro offering a taste of authentic French cuisine. The atmosphere is cozy and inviting, with a focus on simple yet flavorful dishes made from fresh, local ingredients. It's a great spot for a casual lunch or a relaxed dinner, with a menu that caters to a variety of tastes.

Tip: Try their lunch specials, which are not only delicious but also offer great value for money. The outdoor seating is perfect for people-watching and soaking up the local ambiance.

Address: 17 Pl. Victor Hugo, 31000 Toulouse, France
Website: https://la-gourmandine.fr/

CHEZ NAVARRE

Chez Navarre offers a unique dining experience in Toulouse, focusing on communal tables and hearty, traditional Southern French cuisine. The restaurant's rustic charm and warm atmosphere make it a delightful place to share a meal with both friends and strangers. The menu features seasonal, locally-sourced ingredients, ensuring fresh and flavorful dishes.

Tip: Don't miss their cassoulet, a regional specialty. Arriving early or booking ahead is recommended, as the restaurant's communal dining concept makes it a popular spot, especially during dinner hours.
Address: 49 Gd Rue Nazareth, 31000 Toulouse, France
Website: www.chez-navarre.fr

LE BOLI CAFÉ

Le Boli Café is a vibrant and budget-friendly eatery in Toulouse, known for its lively atmosphere and delicious, uncomplicated cuisine. This café is a favorite among locals and students, offering generous portions at affordable prices. The menu includes a variety of dishes, catering to different tastes, including vegetarian options.

Tip: Try their daily specials for a satisfying meal that won't break the bank. The café's relaxed vibe makes it a great spot for a casual lunch or a laid-back evening meal.
Address: 31 Rue Léon Gambetta, 31000 Toulouse, France

Website: www.facebook.com/profile.php?id=100054492907726

CASSOULET TOULOUSAIN

Cassoulet Toulousain is not just a dish; it's a culinary journey into the heart of Toulouse's gastronomic heritage. This rich, slow-cooked stew marries white beans with a variety of meats, typically Toulouse sausage, duck confit, and pork. The slow cooking process infuses the beans with a deep, meaty flavor while tenderizing the meats, resulting in a dish that's both hearty and nuanced. Each spoonful offers a taste of the rustic charm and culinary traditions of the region. It's a dish that comforts the soul and delights the palate. **Where to Try**: "Chez Emile" in Toulouse is renowned for its authentic and flavorful Cassoulet Toulousain.
Location: 13 Pl. Saint-Georges, 31000 Toulouse, France
Tip: Complement your cassoulet with a full-bodied local red wine like a Minervois or Corbières to enhance the dish's rich flavors.

TOULOUSE SAUSAGE - SAUCISSE DE TOULOUSE

Saucisse de Toulouse, a staple of the Toulouse culinary scene, is a testament to the simplicity and excellence of French charcuterie. Made from finely minced pork, seasoned with just the right amount of garlic and pepper, this sausage is celebrated for its delicate texture and robust flavor. It's versatile enough to be the star of a simple grilled meal or an integral component of more complex dishes like Cassoulet Toulousain. When cooked, it releases a mouthwatering aroma and delivers a taste that is unmistakably Toulousain - unpretentious yet utterly satisfying.

Where to Try: Enjoy the authentic taste of Saucisse de Toulouse at "Le Boli Café," a local favorite.
Location: 31 Rue Léon Gambetta, 31000 Toulouse, France
Tip: Pair the sausage with traditional accompaniments like a white bean salad or ratatouille to savor a quintessential Toulousain meal.

FÉNÉTRA

Fénétra, a delightful dessert hailing from Toulouse, embodies the sweet essence of the region. This traditional cake marries the flavors of almonds, lemon, and apricot jam in a tender, airy batter. It's a light yet indulgent treat, distinguished by its bright citrus notes and the sweet tang of apricot, making it a beloved favorite in Toulouse's culinary repertoire. The cake's delicate texture and balanced sweetness make it a perfect conclusion to any meal.

Where to Try: "Pâtisserie Sandyan" in Toulouse offers a delectable version of Fénétra, staying true to its traditional roots.
Location: 54bis Rue d'Alsace Lorraine, 31000 Toulouse, France
Tip: Fénétra pairs excellently with a lightly sweetened tea or a local dessert wine, accentuating its delicate flavors.

VIOLET OF TOULOUSE

The Violet of Toulouse is not just a flower but a symbol of the city's culinary innovation. These candied violets, along with violet-flavored sweets like chocolates and liqueurs, are unique to Toulouse. The use of violets in confectionery is a centuries-old tradition, offering a delicate, floral flavor that is both distinctive and enchanting. These sweets are not only delicious but also visually stunning, making them a popular gift and a must-try delicacy.

Where to Try: "Maison de la Violette" on a barge on the Canal du Midi is renowned for its array of violet-flavored confections.
Location: Sur le Canal du Midi face, 3 Bd Bonrepos, 31000 Toulouse, France
Tip: Try the violet-infused chocolates or liqueurs for a unique taste experience, and consider purchasing some candied violets as a delightful souvenir.

GARBURE

Garbure is a quintessential dish from the Gascony region, which encompasses Toulouse, embodying the heart and soul of local cuisine. This hearty and rustic soup is a confluence of flavors, featuring duck confit, cabbage, and an assortment of root vegetables. Its rich broth, slow-cooked to perfection, is imbued with the depth of . meats and the earthiness of vegetables, creating a comforting and satisfying meal. Garbure is more than just a soup; it's a culinary tradition that speaks to the soul of Southwestern France.

Where to Try: "La Cave au Cassoulet" in Toulouse is known for its authentic and heartwarming Garbure.

Location: 54 Rue Peyrolières, 31000 Toulouse, France

Tip: Enjoy Garbure on a chilly day to experience its warming and nourishing effect fully. Pair it with a local red wine for a sublime culinary experience.

FRONTON WINE

Fronton Wine, from the vineyards just north of Toulouse, is a hidden gem in the world of French wines. Predominantly made from the Negrette grape, unique to this region, Fronton wines are celebrated for their distinct character. These wines, both red and rosé, boast a delightful blend of fruity and spicy notes, making them versatile companions to the robust flavors of Toulouse's cuisine. Tasting Fronton Wine is not just about savoring a drink; it's about immersing oneself in the terroir and tradition of the Toulouse region.

Where to Try: "Vinothèque de Fronton" offers a wide selection of Fronton wines for tasting and purchase.

Location: 140 Allée Du Chateau, 140 Allée du Château BP 15, 31620 Fronton, France

Tip: Pair a glass of Fronton red with a hearty dish like Cassoulet Toulousain or Saucisse de Toulouse to enhance the dining experience. A visit to the vineyards around Fronton can be a delightful excursion from Toulouse.

SHOPPING IN TOULOUSE

MARCHÉ VICTOR HUGO

Marché Victor Hugo is the epitome of a traditional French market, located in the heart of Toulouse. This bustling indoor market is a paradise for food lovers, offering an array of fresh, high-quality produce, meats, cheeses, and seafood. Local vendors also sell a variety of regional specialties and gourmet products. The vibrant atmosphere and the array of tantalizing smells and flavors make it a must-visit for anyone wanting to experience the local culinary scene. **Tip**: Visit the market early in the morning to avoid the crowds and have the best selection of fresh products. Don't miss the chance to have lunch at one of the market's upstairs restaurants, where you can enjoy dishes made from ingredients sourced directly below.
Address: Place Victor Hugo, 31000 Toulouse, France
Website: www.marche-victor-hugo.fr

PLACE SAINT-GEORGES

Place Saint-Georges is not only a picturesque square in Toulouse but also a popular shopping destination. Surrounded by charming buildings, this area hosts a variety of shops ranging from trendy boutiques to well-known fashion brands. It's a great place to find clothing, accessories, and unique gifts. The square also has several cafes and restaurants, making it a perfect spot for a shopping break. **Tip**: Take the time to explore the smaller side streets off Place Saint-Georges, where you can find more unique boutiques and artisan shops. The area becomes especially lively in the evening, with its outdoor dining and vibrant atmosphere. **Address**: Place Saint-Georges, 31000 Toulouse, France. **Website**: www.toulouse-visit.com/marche-place-saint-georges/toulouse/commid031v5013ws

ESPACE SAINT-GEORGES

Espace Saint-Georges is a modern and vibrant shopping center located in the heart of Toulouse. This mall features a wide array of stores, from popular international brands to local retailers. It caters to a variety of shopping needs, including fashion, beauty, and lifestyle products, all in a convenient and accessible location.

Tip: Check out the center's website for special events and promotions. Espace Saint-Georges is not only great for shopping but also offers a range of dining options, perfect for a lunch break or a coffee after a shopping spree.
Address: 51 Rue du Rem Saint-Etienne, 31000 Toulouse, France
Website: www.lesboutiquessaintgeorges.fr

CARRÉ D'ARTISTES

Carré d'Artistes in Toulouse is an inviting art gallery that stands out for making contemporary art accessible to all. This unique space showcases a diverse collection of artworks, including paintings and sculptures, by emerging and established artists. Whether you're an art enthusiast or a casual observer, Carré d'Artistes offers a welcoming environment to explore and purchase original art.

Tip: Don't hesitate to ask the gallery staff for information about the artists or artworks; they are usually very knowledgeable and can enhance your understanding and appreciation of the pieces.

Address: 38 Rue d'Alsace Lorraine, 31000 Toulouse, France
Website: www.carredartistes.com/en-fr/

MARCHÉ AUX PUCES SAINT-AUBIN

The Marché aux Puces Saint-Aubin is a lively flea market in Toulouse, held every Sunday in the Saint-Aubin district. This bustling market is a paradise for bargain hunters and vintage lovers, offering a wide range of items from clothing and accessories to furniture and antiques. It's a great place to find unique and quirky items.

Tip: Arrive early for the best selection of items and be prepared to haggle for the best deals. The market is also a great place to soak up the local atmosphere and enjoy a leisurely Sunday morning.

Address: Boulevard Jules Michelet & Rue Pierre-Paul Riquet
Website: www.facebook.com/saintaubinmarche

GRAINE DE PASTEL

Graine de Pastel in Toulouse is a distinctive store that creatively merges regional heritage with contemporary skincare. Specializing in products made from the pastel plant, once a cornerstone of Toulouse's economy, the boutique offers a range of beauty items imbued with the plant's natural, soothing properties.

From luxurious creams to aromatic soaps, each product tells a story of Toulouse's rich past while catering to modern wellness needs.

Tip: Explore their range of skincare products for a unique, locally-inspired gift or personal indulgence. The pastel body cream is a must-try for its nourishing qualities and connection to Toulouse's history.

Address: 4 Pl. Saint-Étienne, 31000 Toulouse, France
Website: www.grainedepastel.com

FAMILY-FRIENDLY ACTIVITIES IN TOULOUSE

MUSÉUM DE TOULOUSE

The Muséum de Toulouse is one of the essential family-friendly destinations in the city, especially for those interested in natural history and science. This museum offers an extensive collection that includes dinosaur skeletons, mineral displays, and interactive exhibits about the human body and nature. It's an educational and engaging experience for children and adults alike, with hands-on activities and informative displays. **Tip**: Check out the museum's schedule for workshops and special events designed for children, making the visit even more interactive and fun.

Address: 35 All. Jules Guesde, 31000 Toulouse, France
Website: https://museum.toulouse-metropole.fr/en/

ADVENTURE PARK TÉPACAP!

Adventure Park Tépacap! is an outdoor paradise for families looking for an active and adventurous day. Located just outside Toulouse, this park features a range of activities, including tree climbing, zip-lining, and obstacle courses suitable for all ages. It's a perfect place to challenge yourselves and enjoy nature.

Tip: Wear comfortable clothing and closed-toe shoes for the activities. Plan to spend a full day here to take advantage of all the different adventures the park has to offer.

Address: Rte de l'Isle en Dodon, 31370 Rieumes, France
Website: www.tepacap.fr

LE PETIT TRAIN DE TOULOUSE

Le Petit Train de Toulouse offers a charming and leisurely way to explore the city's key attractions. This guided tour aboard a small train is perfect for families, providing a fun and informative ride through the historic streets of Toulouse. It's an ideal activity for those with young children or anyone who wants a quick overview of the city's landmarks.

Tip: Try to grab a seat near the front of the train for the best views and photo opportunities. The tour is especially enjoyable in the late afternoon when the city is bathed in soft light.

Address: Departure from Place du Capitole, 31000 Toulouse, France
Website: https://petittraintoulouse.com/

AFRICAN SAFARI ZOO

The African Safari Zoo, located near Toulouse, is an exciting destination for families. Here, you can discover over 600 animals, including exotic species like lions, giraffes, and rhinos. The zoo offers a unique opportunity to learn about wildlife and their habitats, with both drive-through and walk-through areas.

Tip: Consider visiting early in the morning or late in the afternoon when the animals are most active. Don't miss the educational talks and feeding sessions, which are both entertaining and informative.

Address: 41 Rue des Landes, 31830 Plaisance-du-Touch, France
Website: www.zoo-africansafari.com/en/accueil-en/

ANIMAPARC OCCITANIE

Animaparc Occitanie, nestled near Toulouse, is a delightful blend of an animal park, amusement park, and water park. It's an ideal destination for families, offering a chance to interact with various animals, enjoy fun rides, and splash around in water attractions. The park caters to all ages, making it perfect for a full day of family entertainment.

Tip: Wear comfortable shoes and bring swimsuits for the kids to enjoy the water park section. Visiting on weekdays can help avoid the larger crowds typically present on weekends.

Address: 3000 Pouchot, 31330 Le Burgaud, France
Website: www.animaparc.com

HALLE DE LA MACHINE

Halle de La Machine in Toulouse is a unique museum showcasing extraordinary machines and inventions. This interactive space offers a fascinating and educational experience, where visitors can see and sometimes interact with incredible mechanical creations. It's a place that sparks imagination and creativity, appealing to both children and adults.

Tip: Check the museum's schedule for live demonstrations and shows, where you can see some of the machines in action. These events are particularly captivating and provide a deeper appreciation of the ingenuity behind these creations.

Address: 3 Av. de l'Aérodrome de Montaudran, 31400 Toulouse, France
Website: www.halledelamachine.fr/en

TOULOUSE BY NIGHT
ILLUMINATED MONUMENTS AND EVENING STROLLS
PLACE DU CAPITOLE

Place du Capitole, the heart of Toulouse, transforms into a magical scene at night when its grand façade and surrounding buildings are beautifully illuminated. This historic square, bustling with activity during the day, takes on a more serene and romantic ambiance in the evening. The Capitole building, with its elegant architecture, is particularly stunning when lit up against the night sky. **Tip**: Enjoy a leisurely evening stroll across the square and take in the street performances often found here at night. The area is also surrounded by various cafes and restaurants, perfect for a night-time meal or drink.

Address: Place du Capitole, 31000 Toulouse, France
Website: www.toulouse-visit.com/plaza-hotel-capitole-toulouse/toulouse/hotmid031fs000a9

PONT NEUF

Pont Neuf, Toulouse's oldest bridge, offers a breathtaking sight at night as it lights up over the Garonne River. The illumination highlights its unique structure and arches, creating a picturesque backdrop for an evening walk. The view of the river and the city lights reflecting on the water adds to the enchanting experience.

Tip: For a memorable experience, walk along the riverbanks before crossing the bridge to enjoy the panoramic views of the city. The area is particularly beautiful at sunset and during the early hours of the night.

Address: Pont Neuf, 31000 Toulouse, France
Website: https://en.wikipedia.org/wiki/Pont_Neuf,_Toulouse

QUAI DE LA DAURADE

Quai de la Daurade is a picturesque spot along the Garonne River in Toulouse, known for its stunning views, especially at night. The riverside comes alive with the glow of streetlights and the illuminated reflections on the water, offering a peaceful and romantic setting. It's a favorite amongst locals and tourists for evening strolls, with the majestic backdrop of Toulouse's historic architecture. **Tip**: Bring a camera to capture the beautiful scenery, and consider enjoying a picnic on the riverbank as the city lights sparkle in the background.

Address: Quai de la Daurade, 31000 Toulouse, France
Website: www.toulouse-tournages.fr/la-daurade-quai-place

GARONNE RIVERBANK

The Garonne Riverbank in Toulouse provides a serene and beautiful path for night-time walks. The riverside is beautifully lit, creating a magical atmosphere that enhances the city's charm. The views of the illuminated bridges and historic buildings along the river are particularly striking, making it a perfect spot for an evening stroll.
Tip: For a different perspective, consider a boat tour along the Garonne in the evening. It's a relaxing way to see the city lights and enjoy the tranquil ambiance of the river at night.

Address: Garonne Riverbank, Toulouse, France
Website: www.toulouse-visit.com/heritage-walk-banks-garonne

BARS AND PUBS

LE FROG & ROSBIF

Le Frog & Rosbif, a classic British pub in Toulouse, brings a touch of the UK to the heart of the city. This lively spot is renowned for its selection of craft beers, many of which are brewed on-site. Along with its impressive beer offerings, the pub serves a menu of traditional British pub fare, making it a favorite for both expats and locals. The atmosphere is always vibrant, especially during sports events.

Tip: Try their house-brewed beers for a unique taste experience. The pub is particularly lively during football matches, offering an authentic British pub atmosphere.

Address: 14 Rue de l'Industrie, 31000 Toulouse, France
Website: www.frogpubs.com/pub-the-frog-rosbif-toulouse-toulouse-6.php

LA COULEUR DE LA CULOTTE

La Couleur de la Culotte stands out as a trendy and bustling bar located on the lively Place Saint-Pierre. Known for its fantastic outdoor seating area, it offers stunning views of the Garonne River, making it an ideal spot for an evening out. The bar boasts an extensive drink menu, including local wines and cocktails, catering to a wide range of tastes.

Tip: Grab a seat outside for the best experience, especially during warm evenings. It's a perfect spot for people-watching and soaking in the vibrant atmosphere of Toulouse at night.

Address: 14 Pl. Saint-Pierre, 31000 Toulouse, France
Website: http://www.lacouleurdelaculotte.com/

BAR BASQUE

Bar Basque in Toulouse offers a unique experience with its Basque-themed ambiance. This cozy bar is celebrated for serving a variety of Basque drinks, including regional wines and specialty cocktails, along with delicious pintxos – traditional Basque appetizers. The decor is authentically Basque, creating an inviting and distinctive atmosphere that sets it apart from other bars in the city.

Tip: Don't miss trying the pintxos; they're perfect for sharing and pair wonderfully with the bar's selection of Basque wines.

Address: 7 Pl. Saint-Pierre, 31000 Toulouse, France
Website: www.barbasquetoulouse.fr

THE DANU IRISH PUB

The Danu Irish Pub brings the spirit of Ireland to Toulouse. Known for its friendly environment and traditional Irish pub setting, it offers a wide range of Irish beers and whiskeys. The pub frequently hosts live sports screenings and music nights, making it a lively spot for an evening out. It's a great place to enjoy the camaraderie and charm of an Irish pub.

Tip: Visit on a night with live music for an authentic Irish pub experience. The Danu is also an excellent choice for watching international sports events, offering a fun and vibrant atmosphere.

Address: 9 Rue du Pont Guilheméry, 31000 Toulouse, France
Website: www.thedanu.fr

NIGHTCLUBS AND DANCE CLUBS

LE PURPLE

Le Purple is a prominent nightclub in Toulouse, celebrated for its lively atmosphere and a diverse selection of music. The club attracts a young and energetic crowd, ready to dance to the latest hits, electronic beats, and occasional themed nights. The vibrant lighting and state-of-the-art sound system enhance the clubbing experience, making it a popular choice for a night out in the city.

Tip: Check their social media pages for information on special events or guest DJs to plan your visit for a night full of energy and entertainment.

Address: 2 Rue Castellane, 31000 Toulouse, France
Website: http://www.purepurple.fr/dev/

LA DYNAMO

La Dynamo stands out in Toulouse's nightlife scene for its eclectic programming and intimate setting. This club is a hub for music lovers, offering everything from electronic to indie genres, along with regular live performances and DJ sets. The atmosphere is both vibrant and welcoming, catering to a crowd that appreciates a variety of music styles in a more personal venue.

Tip: Arrive early to enjoy a more relaxed atmosphere before the night heats up. Keep an eye on their schedule for live music nights, which are a particular highlight at La Dynamo.

Address: 6 Rue Amélie, 31000 Toulouse, France
Website: www.facebook.com/lasaintedynamo/

CLUB LE SAINT DES SEINS

Club Le Saint des Seins, nestled in the vibrant Place Saint-Pierre, is a dynamic venue in Toulouse known for its diverse music scene. This club, popular with the younger crowd, hosts a variety of music genres, ranging from rock to electronic. The energetic atmosphere, coupled with regular live music and DJ nights, makes it a go-to spot for those seeking a lively night out.

Tip: Be sure to catch one of their live music nights for an unforgettable experience that showcases local and upcoming talent.
Address: 5 Pl. Saint-Pierre, 31000 Toulouse, France
Website: www.instagram.com/lesaintdesseins_official/

LE CRI DE LA MOUETTE

Le Cri de la Mouette is a unique maritime-themed nightclub in Toulouse, offering a diverse and vibrant night out. Known for its quirky decor and varied music offerings, the club hosts themed nights and DJ sets that cater to a wide array of musical tastes. This energetic spot is perfect for those who enjoy an eclectic mix of mainstream and underground beats.

Tip: Check out their themed nights for a special experience – each event offers a different vibe and music style, ensuring a unique visit every time.
Address: 78 All. de Barcelone, 31000 Toulouse, France
Website: www.facebook.com/lecridelamouette/

LATE-NIGHT DINING

LE BISTROT DES HALLES

Le Bistrot des Halles, located near the vibrant Marché Victor Hugo, is an excellent choice for late-night dining in Toulouse. This charming bistro offers a range of traditional French dishes, known for their rich flavors and generous portions. The atmosphere here is both cozy and welcoming, making it a perfect spot for a relaxed dinner after exploring the city at night.

Tip: Try their regional specialties, which are made with fresh ingredients sourced from the nearby market. Be sure to save room for their delectable desserts.

Address: 17 Pl. Roguet, 31300 Toulouse, France
Website: www.instagram.com/lebistrotdeshalles_tlse/

LA FAIM DES HARICOTS

La Faim des Haricots is a gem in Toulouse for vegetarians and vegans, offering a diverse and tasty menu that caters to a late-night crowd. Their dishes range from hearty salads to innovative main courses, all prepared with fresh, quality ingredients. The restaurant's warm and inviting ambiance adds to its charm, making it a popular choice for a late meal.

Tip: Don't miss their daily specials, which often feature creative and seasonal vegan and vegetarian dishes.

Address: 2bis Rue du Puits Vert, 31000 Toulouse, France
Website: www.lafaimdesharicots.fr

L'ENTRECÔTE

L'Entrecôte in Toulouse is a bustling steakhouse, renowned for its simple yet irresistible menu. The restaurant's signature dish is a walnut salad followed by tender steak, sliced thin, and served with a secret sauce and unlimited fries. The lively atmosphere and efficient service make it an ideal spot for late-night dining, especially for meat lovers.

Tip: Arrive early or be prepared for a wait, as the restaurant's popularity means it's often busy. The steak is the star here, so we recommend focusing on enjoying this classic dish.
Address: 15 Bd de Strasbourg, 31000 Toulouse, France
Website: www.entrecote.fr

LES 4 Z'ARTS

Les 4 Z'Arts, nestled in the heart of Toulouse, is a cozy bistro offering a diverse selection of local and international dishes. Its relaxed atmosphere and late-night service make it a wonderful choice for those looking to wind down after an evening out. The menu caters to a variety of tastes, ensuring there's something for everyone.

Tip: Try one of their local dishes for a taste of regional cuisine, or opt for one of their creative cocktails to accompany your meal. The bistro's intimate setting is perfect for a quieter, more relaxed dining experience.
Address: 11 Pl. de la Daurade, 31000 Toulouse, France
Website: www.facebook.com/p/Les-4-zarts-100063756903980/

NIGHTLIFE AREAS

PLACE SAINT-PIERRE

Place Saint-Pierre is the pulsating heart of Toulouse's nightlife, especially known among students and young locals. This lively square is lined with an array of bars and pubs, each offering a unique ambiance, from cozy to party-centric. The open-air setting by the Garonne River adds to its charm, making it a perfect spot for socializing and enjoying the vibrant atmosphere. The area buzzes with energy, particularly on weekends, as crowds gather to enjoy drinks and music.

Tip: Try to explore multiple bars here to fully experience the diverse vibes. The terrace of La Couleur de la Culotte offers excellent views and is a popular spot to start the evening.

Address: Place Saint-Pierre, 31000 Toulouse, France

RUE GABRIEL PÉRI

Rue Gabriel Péri is a dynamic and trendy street in Toulouse, bustling with a youthful crowd looking to enjoy the night. Lined with a variety of bars, clubs, and late-night eateries, this street caters to an eclectic mix of tastes and styles. From intimate jazz bars to lively dance clubs, Rue Gabriel Péri offers a slice of Toulouse's diverse nightlife, all within a walkable stretch.

Tip: Visit Le Moloko for a taste of its unique cocktails in a retro-futuristic setting. If you're in the mood for dancing, Le Purple nightclub on this street is a must-visit for its energetic atmosphere.

Address: Rue Gabriel Péri, 31000 Toulouse, France

LE QUARTIER DES CARMES

Le Quartier des Carmes in Toulouse is a charming and sophisticated area, renowned for its vibrant nightlife. This neighborhood seamlessly blends the old-world charm of Toulouse with a modern and lively ambiance. Filled with an assortment of bars, chic restaurants, and trendy nightspots, it's a favorite haunt for those seeking an elegant yet exciting night out. The area's narrow streets and historic architecture provide a picturesque backdrop for the bustling cafes and vibrant terraces.

Tip: Explore the small side streets to discover hidden bars and cozy bistros that offer a more intimate atmosphere. Don't miss trying some local wine or a cocktail at one of the stylish bars.

Address: Quartier des Carmes, 31000 Toulouse, France

JEAN JAURÈS

The Jean Jaurès area in Toulouse, known for its wide boulevard and surrounding streets, is a popular destination for nightlife. It offers a dynamic and varied scene, with a plethora of bars, pubs, and late-night eateries catering to all tastes. Whether you're looking for a laid-back pub, a lively bar with live music, or a place to dance the night away, Jean Jaurès has it all. The area's central location makes it a bustling hub for both locals and visitors.

Tip: Head to one of the rooftop bars in the area for a spectacular view of Toulouse at night. For a unique experience, check out the themed bars along the boulevard, each offering a different ambiance and specialty drinks.

Address: Allées Jean Jaurès, 31000 Toulouse, France

SAFETY TIPS

Exploring Toulouse by night can be an exhilarating experience, but it's important to prioritize your safety to ensure your evening adventures remain pleasant memories. Here are some safety tips to keep in mind:

- **Vigilance is key**: Crowded venues and bustling streets are prime spots for pickpockets. Always be mindful of your personal belongings and consider using anti-theft bags or pouches.
- **Stay in the light**: Stick to well-lit and populated streets, especially if you're venturing out alone. Dark and deserted alleys can be risky, so it's best to avoid them.
- **Trustworthy transport**: Use only reputable taxi companies or verified ride-sharing apps for nighttime travel. It's wise to pre-save the contact details of a reliable taxi service on your phone.
- **Guard your glass**: While enjoying the local nightlife, never leave your drink unattended. Accept beverages only from trusted companions or directly from the bartender.
- **Drink smart**: Consume alcohol in moderation and stay hydrated with water throughout the night. This will help you maintain awareness and make better decisions.
- **Emergency preparedness**: Keep a list of emergency contacts, including local authorities and your embassy, easily accessible. A portable phone charger can be a lifesaver in keeping your device powered up.
- **Document safety**: Carry photocopies of your essential documents, such as your passport, and store the originals in a secure location like a hotel safe.

Remember, the night is yours to enjoy, but staying alert and prepared is the best way to ensure that your nocturnal explorations are safe and enjoyable.

By following these tips and exploring the city by night, you'll be able to experience the magic and charm of the city while staying safe and having an unforgettable time.

ART, HISTORY AND ARCHITECTURE

Toulouse: A Canvas of Art, History, and Architectural Elegance

Toulouse, known as "La Ville Rose" (The Pink City) for its distinctive terracotta brickwork, stands as a testament to the harmonious blend of art, history, and architecture in southwestern France. This historic city, with its roots in the Roman era, has evolved from a prosperous medieval trading center to a hub of aerospace and technological innovation.

At the heart of Toulouse's artistic legacy is its rich medieval and Renaissance past, reflected in its impressive collection of art and architecture. The Basilica of Saint-Sernin, a masterpiece of Romanesque architecture and a key stop on the pilgrimage route to Santiago de Compostela, houses exquisite relics and artworks. The Musée des Augustins, with its extensive collection of sculptures and paintings, showcases the city's artistic evolution from the Middle Ages to the modern era.

Historically, Toulouse played a pivotal role in the region, especially during the Albigensian Crusade in the 13th century. Its history is intricately linked with the Occitan culture, which is celebrated in the city's museums and cultural events. The Capitole de Toulouse, the city's town hall and opera house, stands as a symbol of its civic pride and architectural splendor.

Architecturally, Toulouse is a blend of historical and modern styles. The city's layout, characterized by narrow medieval streets and expansive public squares, is punctuated by grandiose structures like the Pont Neuf and the modernist architecture of the Cité de l'Espace, reflecting its status as a European aerospace hub.

Toulouse's commitment to preserving its cultural heritage while embracing modernity is evident in its vibrant arts scene, including contemporary galleries and theaters. The city's culinary offerings, from traditional Occitan dishes to innovative cuisine, mirror its rich cultural tapestry.

Today, Toulouse stands as a city where history, art, and architecture intertwine in an elegant dance. Each street, building, and artwork tells a story, weaving a rich tapestry of cultural heritage. For those seeking a journey through time, culture, and creativity, Toulouse offers an experience like no other.

ART AND CULTURE IN TOULOUSE

THÉÂTRE DU CAPITOLE

The Théâtre du Capitole, nestled in the vibrant heart of Toulouse, is a beacon of the city's rich cultural and artistic heritage. This historic theater, with its majestic façade and opulent interiors, is a symbol of elegance and sophistication. Renowned for its world-class opera and ballet performances, the theater's plush red seating, ornate decorations, and grand chandeliers set the scene for an unforgettable artistic experience. The Théâtre du Capitole's program presents a harmonious blend of classic masterpieces and innovative contemporary works, showcasing the talents of internationally acclaimed artists as well as emerging stars in the realms of opera and ballet. Each performance is a display of impeccable artistry, complemented by stunning stage designs and enchanting orchestral music, ensuring a truly mesmerizing experience for the audience.

Tip: For a more enriching experience, partake in the theater's pre-show talks or guided tours, offering valuable insights into its historic significance and current productions. It's advisable to book tickets well in advance, as performances often sell out quickly. Completing a visit with a stroll through the adjacent Place du Capitole, especially after an evening show, is highly recommended. This bustling area, with its numerous dining options and lively atmosphere, perfectly encapsulates the essence of Toulouse's vibrant cultural scene.

Address: Pl. du Capitole, 31000 Toulouse, France
Website: https://opera.toulouse.fr/

MUSÉE DE LA RÉSISTANCE ET DE LA DÉPORTATION

The Musée de la Résistance et de la Déportation in Toulouse offers a poignant look into the French Resistance and the experiences of deportees during World War II. This museum houses a significant collection of documents, photographs, and artifacts that narrate the story of resistance, occupation, and liberation. It's an essential visit for those interested in history and the human spirit's resilience. **Tip**: Allocate enough time for your visit, as the museum provides a comprehensive and moving experience. The audio guides available are highly recommended for a deeper understanding of the exhibits.
Address: 52 Allée des Demoiselles, 31400 Toulouse, France
Website: www.facebook.com/museeresistance.hautegaronne

CINÉMATHÈQUE DE TOULOUSE

The Cinémathèque de Toulouse is a paradise for film enthusiasts. This institution is dedicated to the preservation and showcasing of cinema, with a vast archive of films from all over the world. It hosts screenings, retrospectives, and film-related events, making it a vibrant center for cinematic culture. The Cinémathèque also organizes workshops and educational programs, contributing to the appreciation of film as an art form.
Tip: Check their schedule before visiting to catch special screenings or thematic film festivals. The experience of watching a classic film in their vintage theater is not to be missed.
Address: 69 Rue du Taur, 31000 Toulouse, France
Website: www.lacinemathequedetoulouse.com

L'USINE À MUSIQUE

L'Usine à Musique in Toulouse is a vibrant hub for contemporary music and cultural events. This unique venue is known for its eclectic programming, featuring everything from rock and electronic to indie music. It's a space where local bands and international acts alike take the stage, offering an exciting mix of live performances. The atmosphere here is electric, making it a favorite spot for music lovers and night owls.

Tip: Keep an eye on their event calendar for themed music nights or special concerts. It's a great place to discover new artists and enjoy a night of diverse musical offerings.

Address: Rue Louis Bonin, 31200 Toulouse, France
Website: www.lusineamusique.fr

CENTRE DE L'AFFICHE

The Centre de l'Affiche in Toulouse is dedicated to the fascinating world of posters and graphic arts. This unique museum houses a vast collection of vintage and contemporary posters, showcasing the evolution of graphic design and advertising. Visitors can explore various themes, from political and cultural movements to artistic trends, all through the lens of poster art.

Tip: The museum often hosts temporary exhibitions, so check their schedule for current displays. It's a perfect visit for design enthusiasts and those interested in visual communication.

Address: 58 All. Charles de Fitte, 31300 Toulouse, France
Website: www.facebook.com/MATOU.Musee/

MUSÉE PAUL DUPUY

The Musée Paul Dupuy is a hidden gem in Toulouse, specializing in decorative arts and graphic arts. Its collection spans from the Middle Ages to the early 20th century, featuring an impressive array of drawings, watches, and fine art objects. The museum, set in an elegant mansion, offers a journey through time, showcasing the evolution of artistic styles and craftsmanship. It's a must-visit for those interested in the intricacies of art history and design.

Tip: Don't miss the collection of historical timepieces, which is one of the highlights of the museum. Their intricate designs and craftsmanship are truly fascinating.

Address: 13 Rue de la Pleau, 31000 Toulouse, France
Website: https://museepauldupuy.toulouse.fr/

SALLE DES ILLUSTRES AT THE CAPITOLE

Nestled within Toulouse's grand Capitole building, the Salle des Illustres is a testament to the city's cultural legacy. This ornate hall, lined with exquisite art, reflects the historical milestones and notable personalities of Toulouse. The elaborate ceiling, intricate frescoes, and classical sculptures create an atmosphere of awe, transporting visitors back in time.

Tip: To best experience the Salle des Illustres, plan your visit to coincide with the Capitole's open days or special events, when the hall is often open to the public. This allows for a more in-depth exploration of both the Salle des Illustres and the Capitole's other historic rooms.

Address: Place du Capitole, 31000 Toulouse, France
Website: www.toulouse-visit.com/le-capitole

HISTORICAL AND ARCHITECTURAL LANDMARKS IN TOULOUSE
CÚPULA DE LA GRAVE

The Chapelle Saint Joseph de La Grave is a prominent historical landmark in Toulouse, situated elegantly along the Garonne River. Originally part of La Grave Hospital, established in 1197 for plague victims, it played a significant role in the city's healthcare history. During the 17th century, the chapel became central to the Great Imprisonment of the poor, hosting workshops that trained the needy in artisanal skills.

The chapel is most notable for its stunning 18th-century dome, a masterpiece of classical French architecture that dominates Toulouse's skyline. This architectural gem symbolizes Toulouse's commitment to social welfare and architectural excellence.

Tip: While exploring the chapel's interior, visitors can appreciate the intricate architecture and understand its historical significance in social aid. The Pont Saint-Pierre nearby offers a splendid viewpoint, especially during sunset. The golden hour light beautifully illuminates the chapel and river, providing a perfect backdrop for photographers and an immersive historical experience for all visitors.

Address: Rue du Pont Saint-Pierre, 31300 Toulouse, France
Website: www.toulouse-visit.com/chapelle-saint-joseph-de-la-grave/toulouse/pcumid031v50160o

BASILIQUE DE LA DAURADE

Basilique de la Daurade, nestled along the Garonne River, is a revered historical basilica in Toulouse. Known for housing the Black Virgin statue, the basilica is an important religious site with significant art pieces. Its history dates back to Roman times, evolving through various architectural changes.

Tip: Take time to explore the interior of the basilica, especially the revered Black Virgin statue. The riverside location offers a peaceful setting, ideal for a reflective stroll along the Garonne.

Address: 1 Place de la Daurade, 31000 Toulouse, France

Website: www.toulouse-visit.com/basilique-notre-dame-de-la-daurade/toulouse/pcumid031fs00961

RAYMOND VI GARDEN

Raymond VI Garden, nestled near Toulouse's Garonne River, is a peaceful sanctuary rich in history. It's not just a spot for relaxation but also a window into the city's Roman and medieval past. Named after Count Raymond VI of Toulouse, it stands where he famously crossed the Garonne upon returning from exile. The garden's lush lawns and ancient ruins provide a tranquil escape and an educational experience. It's an ideal place for history buffs and those seeking quietude.

Tip: Stroll through the garden for a serene experience, perfect for a quiet picnic or a thoughtful walk, especially in warmer months. The garden's riverside location also offers picturesque city views.

Address: Allée Charles de Fitte, 31300 Toulouse, France

Website: www.toulouse-visit.com/jardin-raymond-vi/toulouse/pcumid031fs0007c

PONT SAINT-PIERRE

The Pont Saint-Pierre in Toulouse is a striking bridge that offers picturesque views of the Garonne River and city skyline. Connecting the city center to its southern bank, the bridge symbolizes Toulouse's urban development and is a popular spot for both locals and tourists, especially at sunset.

Tip: For the best experience, visit the bridge at dusk to witness the stunning sunset over the river. It's also an ideal spot for photographers looking to capture the beauty of Toulouse, with the river and city as a backdrop.

Address: Pont Saint-Pierre, 31000 Toulouse, France
Website: https://fr.wikipedia.org/wiki/Pont_Saint-Pierre_de_Toulouse

QUARTIER SAINT-ÉTIENNE

The Quartier Saint-Étienne is the historic heart of Toulouse, known for its medieval architecture and narrow, cobblestone streets. This area is home to the impressive Saint-Étienne Cathedral and numerous charming shops and cafes. It's a window into the city's rich past, offering a picturesque stroll through history.

Tip: Wander around the quarter to discover hidden courtyards and artisan boutiques. Don't miss the Saint-Étienne Cathedral, a stunning example of Gothic architecture.

Address: Quartier Saint-Étienne, 31000 Toulouse, France
Website: www.toulouse-visit.com/emblematic-quarters

LE COUVENT DES RÉCOLLETS

Le Couvent des Récollets, a former convent in Toulouse, now serves as a cultural and community space. Its serene cloister and classic architectural features offer a peaceful retreat from the bustling city. The convent reflects Toulouse's religious history and architectural evolution.

Tip: Visit during one of the many cultural events or exhibitions often held here to experience the blend of historical ambiance and contemporary creativity. The cloister is particularly beautiful in the spring and summer months.

Address: 36 Boulevard des Récollets, 31000 Toulouse, France
Website: https://ep-saintegermaine-saintemariedesanges.fr/

PALAIS NIEL

Palais Niel in Toulouse, an architectural gem, serves as the headquarters of the Army's 11th Parachute Brigade. This 19th-century mansion is a striking example of Second Empire architecture, characterized by its ornate facades and elegant interiors.

The building reflects the military history and architectural grandeur of the city.

Tip: While Palais Niel is not typically open to the public, its exterior is worth admiring for architecture enthusiasts. The annual Heritage Days might offer a rare opportunity for a closer look inside.

Address: Rue Montoulieu Saint-Jacques, 31000 Toulouse
Website: https://fr.wikipedia.org/wiki/Palais_Niel

DAY TRIPS FROM TOULOUSE

ALBI

Located just 85 kilometers northeast of Toulouse, is a UNESCO World Heritage site famous for its red-brick architecture. This town is home to the majestic Sainte-Cécile Cathedral, the world's largest brick cathedral, and the Berbie Palace, housing the Toulouse-Lautrec Museum. Old Alby, the historic center, features medieval neighborhoods and Renaissance courtyards. Getting There: Reach Albi by train or car from Toulouse, with a train journey taking about 1 hour. **Tip**: Enjoy a walk through the old town and by the Tarn River, and don't miss the panoramic views from the Grand Théâtre les Cordeliers.
Website: www.albi-tourisme.fr/en/

CARCASSONNE

Carcassonne, about 90 kilometers southeast of Toulouse, is a UNESCO World Heritage medieval fortress town. It features double-walled fortifications and 53 towers. The Cité de Carcassonne offers narrow, cobbled streets, a Gothic cathedral, and historical insights. Highlights include the Basilica of Saints Nazarius and Celsus with stunning stained glass. Getting There: Carcassonne is accessible by train from Toulouse in about an hour. **Tip**: Opt for a guided tour for an immersive historical experience. The fortress is particularly enchanting in the evening when lit up.
Website: www.tourisme-carcassonne.fr/en/

MOISSAC

Moissac, renowned for its Abbey Saint-Pierre, a UNESCO World Heritage Site, offers a blend of spiritual heritage and picturesque charm. This quaint town is known for its remarkable cloister and church, showcasing exquisite Romanesque art and architecture. Stroll through the old streets, and you'll be enchanted by the peaceful ambiance and historic beauty. The abbey's museum adds depth to the visit, revealing the town's rich history.
Getting There: Moissac is accessible via a comfortable drive or train journey from Toulouse. **Tip**: Don't miss the opportunity to explore the abbey's cloister, famous for its beautifully sculpted capitals. The nearby Tarn River also offers scenic walking paths.
Website: www.tourisme-moissac-terresdesconfluences.fr/en

LOURDES

Lourdes, a global center of Marian pilgrimage, welcomes millions of visitors yearly, drawn to its spiritual significance and serene ambiance. The Sanctuary of Our Lady of Lourdes, with the Grotto of Massabielle, is the focal point, where pilgrims seek hope and healing. Beyond the spiritual sites, Lourdes offers stunning natural landscapes, including the nearby Pyrenees mountains.
Getting There: Lourdes is a short train ride or drive from Toulouse, making it an easily accessible destination.
Tip: While the Sanctuary is a must-visit, also explore the town's charming streets and the surrounding natural beauty for a complete experience.
Website: https://en.lourdes-infotourisme.com/

GAILLAC WINE ROUTE

Gaillac Wine Route, 50 kilometers northeast of Toulouse, is a haven for wine lovers. Explore one of France's oldest wine regions, known for its unique local grape varieties and diverse wines. This scenic route winds through vineyards and historic villages, inviting visits to various wineries for tastings. The area features charming wine cellars and cooperative wineries, each showcasing its unique flavors. **Getting There**: The best way to discover the Gaillac Wine Route is by car.
Tip: Arrange tastings and tours at different wineries to learn about the wine-making process and regional history. Many offer local gastronomic delights, perfect for wine pairing.
Website: www.la-toscane-occitane.com/en/

RIEUX-VOLVESTRE

Rieux-Volvestre, located 43 kilometers southwest of Toulouse, offers a journey back in time. This medieval town, nestled on the banks of the Garonne River, boasts beautifully preserved architecture, including a 16th-century cathedral and the Palais des Evêques. Walking through its narrow streets, you'll discover charming half-timbered houses, artisanal shops, and quaint cafes. The town's serene riverside setting provides a peaceful retreat. **Getting There**: Rieux-Volvestre can be reached by car or by regional bus services from Toulouse.
Tip: Don't miss the local market for a taste of regional specialties and a chance to mingle with the locals.
Website: https://tourisme.volvestre.fr/home/

NAJAC

Najac, nestled in the Aveyron region about 75 kilometers northeast of Toulouse, is a breathtaking medieval village. Famous for its imposing Najac Castle, the village offers panoramic views of the Aveyron Valley. The picturesque streets, lined with ancient stone houses, create a serene, historic atmosphere.

Getting There: The drive from Toulouse to Najac takes around 1.5 hours. Alternatively, you can take a train journey of approximately 2 hours.

Tip: Explore Najac Castle for its historical significance. Also, visit local artisan shops and try the regional cuisine for an authentic experience.

Website: www.tourisme-aveyron.com/en/discover/najac/discover-najac-touristic-guide-najac

SAINT GIRONS

Saint Girons, located in the Ariège department roughly 100 kilometers southwest of Toulouse, is a charming town set against the backdrop of the Pyrenees. This town is renowned for its vibrant Saturday market, offering local produce and crafts. Its streets are lined with colorful houses and inviting cafes.

Getting There: A scenic 1.5-hour drive from Toulouse will get you to Saint Girons.

Tip: Visit on a Saturday to experience the lively local market. The surrounding area is also great for outdoor activities like hiking and cycling.

Website: www.ariegepyrenees.com/en/to-prepare/explorer/villages/saint-girons/

ANDORRA

Andorra, a small yet striking principality nestled between France and Spain in the Pyrenees mountains, lies about 185 kilometers from Toulouse. Famous for its ski resorts, duty-free shopping, and stunning natural beauty, Andorra offers a perfect mix of adventure and relaxation.
The capital, Andorra la Vella, is renowned for its bustling commercial centers and vibrant culture.
Getting There: A scenic 3-hour drive from Toulouse.
Tip: Explore the hiking trails in summer and visit the Caldea Spa, Europe's largest spa complex, for a unique experience.
Website: https://visitandorra.com/en/

CORDES-SUR-CIEL

Nestled about 85 kilometers northeast of Toulouse, Cordes-sur-Ciel is a medieval hilltop town that appears to float above the clouds on misty mornings. This enchanting town is known for its breathtaking views, historic Gothic architecture, and cobblestone streets lined with art galleries and artisan shops. A visit here is a step back in time.
Getting There: A drive of approximately 1.5 hours from Toulouse.
Tip: Make sure to visit the Musée d'Art Moderne et Contemporain and enjoy local cafes for regional delicacies.

Website: www.la-toscane-occitane.com/en/towns-villages/cordes-sur-ciel

END NOTE

As we conclude our journey through the enchanting city of Toulouse, it's evident that this vibrant metropolis in the heart of France's southwest region is a treasure trove of culture, history, and culinary delights. Known as 'La Ville Rose' for its distinctive terracotta brick architecture, Toulouse offers a unique blend of ancient allure and modern dynamism.

Toulouse's rich history, dating back to Roman times, is palpable in its historic landmarks and picturesque streets. The city's commitment to preserving its heritage while embracing the future is evident in its well-preserved historical sites and state-of-the-art space exploration facilities. The Basilique Saint-Sernin, a jewel of Romanesque art, and the Capitole, the city's bustling heart, are testimonies to Toulouse's glorious past. Meanwhile, the Cité de l'Espace opens a window to the cosmos, reflecting the city's leading role in the aerospace industry.

The city's culinary scene is as diverse as it is flavorful. From the hearty traditional cassoulet to the innovative creations in Michelin-starred restaurants, Toulouse caters to every palate. Local markets brimming with fresh produce, artisanal cheeses, and regional wines are a gastronome's paradise. The city's bars and pubs, from traditional French bistros to lively Irish pubs, offer a vibrant nightlife scene that's both welcoming and exciting.

Toulouse's cultural tapestry is rich and varied. Art and culture enthusiasts will find a plethora of museums, galleries, and theaters showcasing everything from ancient artifacts to contemporary artworks and performing arts. The city's love for rugby is palpable, with the local team, Stade Toulousain, enjoying a passionate following.

For those seeking tranquility, Toulouse's parks and gardens offer lush green spaces perfect for relaxation and leisure. The banks of the Garonne River and the Canal du Midi provide picturesque settings for leisurely strolls and bike rides.

Nearby, the region offers a variety of day trips, from the historic city of Albi to the stunning medieval fortress of Carcassonne. The surrounding countryside, with its vineyards and charming villages, offers a peaceful escape from city life.

In closing, Toulouse is a city that appeals to all senses and interests. Whether you're a history buff, a foodie, an art lover, or simply seeking a charming French experience, Toulouse is a destination that will leave you enriched and longing to return. As you explore its streets and meet its people, you'll understand why Toulouse is not just a city to visit but an experience to savor.

Bon voyage et bonnes découvertes!

EXTRA RESOURCES

Toulouse maps

Toulouse Detailed Street Map

Toulouse Tourist Map

Toulouse Sightseeing Map

Toulouse Bike Lanes Map

Toulouse Transport Map

Toulouse Metro and Tam Map

Bike-sharing Toulouse

Tisséo (Public Transport in Toulouse)

Toulouse Tourism Office

Toulouse City Pass

TRAVEL

PLACES TO SEE:

LOCAL FOOD TO TRY:

DAY 1
DAY 2
DAY 3
DAY 4
DAY 5
DAY 6

NOTES

PLANNER

★★★★★

Loved Your Journey With Our Guide?

Your feedback makes a world of difference! If our guide helped you, we would be thrilled if you could take a moment to leave us a 5-star review on our product page.

Simply click the link or go to any of our product pages on your preferred retailer website and **share your recommendations.**
https://www.amazon.com/stores/Tailored-Travel-Guides/author/B0C4TV5TZX

Scan the QR Code to share your recommendations

Join our Tailored Travel Guides Network
for more benefits by accessing this link:
https://mailchi.mp/d151cba349e8/ttgnetwork
Or by scanning the QR code

Thank you for chosing Tailored Travel Guides!

GUIDES

Discover Your Journey

UNLOCK A WORLD OF UNFORGETTABLE EXPERIENCES WITH TAILORED TRAVEL GUIDES!

As your go-to source for personalized and meticulously crafted travel guides, we ensure that every adventure is uniquely yours. Our team of dedicated travel experts and local insiders design each guide with your preferences, interests, and travel style in mind, providing you with the ultimate customized travel experience.

Embark on your next journey with confidence, knowing that Tailored Travel Guides has got you covered. To explore more exceptional destinations and discover a treasure trove of additional guides, visit www.tailoredtravelguides.com. or our collection available on:

Amazon at this link: www.amazon.com/stores/Tailored-Travel-Guides/author/B0C4TV5TZX or
on **Google Play**, at this link: https://play.google.com/store/books/author?id=Tailored+Travel+Guides
on **Etsy**, at this link: https://tailoredtravelguides.etsy.com

Happy travels, and here's to a lifetime of remarkable memories!

ALSO IN THE SERIES

Marseille

Nantes

Toulouse

Nice

Paris

Lille

Lyon

Montpellier

Bordeaux

Strasbourg

CHECK OUT THE ITALY UNCOVERED SERIES

Turin	Bologna
Rome	Milan
Genoa	Venice
Verona	Florence
Naples	Palermo

CHECK OUT THE SPAIN UNVEILED SERIES

Malaga

Valencia

Cordoba

Toledo

Madrid

Granada

Barcelona

Seville

Bilbao

San Sebastian

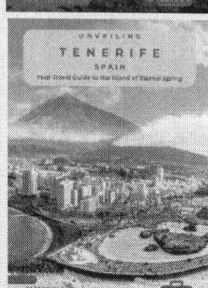

Tenerife

Printed in Great Britain
by Amazon